1   Land and Sea: one foot on deck,
    one hand on the plough

2   *Next page* Dock, later known as Devonport, was first established as a naval base at the end of the seventeenth century; at one time the town became even larger than Plymouth. The massive *Duke of Wellington* lies in Queen's Dock, Keyham, Devonport. A few months after the calotype was made she was in action in the Baltic. She carried 131 guns, and a crew of 1,100 – the first three-decker to fly the British flag. Calotype: Linnaeus Tripe, 1855

Victorian and Edwardian

DEVON

from old photographs

Introduction and commentaries by
BRIAN CHUGG

B.T.Batsford Ltd.
LONDON AND SYDNEY

In memory of John Chugg: Master Mariner

B. T. Batsford Limited
4 Fitzhardinge Street, London W1H 0AH
and 23 Cross Street, Brookvale, N.S.W. 2100, Australia

Phototypeset by Tradespools Ltd, Frome, Somerset
Printed in Great Britain by
The Anchor Press, Tiptree, Essex

First published in 1975
Text copyright © Brian Chugg

ISBN 0 7134 3001 X

CONTENTS

3   Cleaning shot at the Gunwharf, Devonport. Cannon balls were cleaned to give them greater accuracy when fired. A stack of polished balls can be seen between the two men on the left; behind the tree there are two rows of cannon barrels. At this date the army supplied the navy with its ordnance requirements. Calotype: Linnaeus Tripe, 1855

Acknowledgements   vi   Notes on photographers   xii
Introduction   vii

ILLUSTRATION NUMBER

Early photographs of Devon   1–6   South Devon   57–69
The Devon Scene   7–9   The Land   70–85
The Cities   The Sea   86–103
   Exeter   10–14   Dartmoor   104–114
   Plymouth   15–24   The New Machines   115–129
Community Life   25–45   Visitors   130–140
Great Events   46–56   North Devon   141–155

ACKNOWLEDGEMENTS

The Author's warm thanks are due to Professor W. G. Hoskins for his encouragement, and to Dr Robert Newton for his thoughtful comments and practical suggestions which have been used freely. Particular thanks are due to Mr C. P. Stone of Exeter City Library for introducing the Author to the work of A. W. Searley and J. Stabb, and for much help and advice. Mr Stephen Knight of Barnstaple is thanked for his sustained patience in getting the most out of many old photographs.

Photographic Sources: This book could not have been produced without the help of many organisations and individuals. The publishers and Author are most grateful to them for allowing copies to be made of photographs in their collections and for the photographs which have been finally selected they wish to thank: The Beaford Centre Photographic Archive (33, 41, 44, 46, 54, 71, 77, 79); Bideford Museum (27, 30, 36, 38); Brixham Museum (48, 99, 116); Budleigh Salterton Arts Centre and Museum (25, 26, 52); Mrs Eileen Cooper (135); Devon County Library, Headquarters (101); Devon Record Office (74, 75, 81, 104, 109); Exeter City Library (12, 28, 29, 34, 42, 51, 61, 66, 67, 68, 69, 72, 80, 84, 87, 88, 89, 98, 100, 102, 105, 107, 110, 112, 125, 132, 138, 143, 149, 150); Exeter Record Office (10, 11, 115, 126); Exmoor Society (124); Holsworthy Museum (56); Mr B. D. Hughes (45); Ilfracombe Museum (31, 35, 76, 136, 137, 146, 147, 154); International Museum of Photography, New York (139); Messrs R. L. Knight (119, 121, 122); Lockyer Street Hospital, Plymouth (32); Lundy Museum Photographic Archive (153); Mr R. M. Marks (114); Museum of English Rural Life, University of Reading (7, 70, 152); Mr B. J. Nash (55); Mrs M. A. Nash (153); National Maritime Museum (4, 5, 86, 91, 92, 93, 95, 103, 148); North Devon Athenaeum (85, 142, 144); Plymouth City Museum and Art Gallery (2, 3, 21, 22, 23); Plymouth City Reference Library (15, 16, 17, 18, 19, 20, 24, 96); Rothman Collection of Photographs by F. Frith (151); Lady S. Sayer (9, 37, 50, 106, 108, 111, 120); Science Museum (47); Sidmouth Museum (73, 94); South Molton Museum (53, 82); Torbay Aircraft Museum (127); Torquay Central Library (39, 63, 97, 117, 128); Torquay Natural History Society Museum (6, 40, 49, 58, 60, 78, 113); Torrington and District Society (145); Totnes Museum (59); Victoria and Albert Museum (14, 131); Mr R. B. Wright (43). The remaining photographs are from the Publisher's collection.

Local government reorganisation occurred during the course of work on this book and the names of some libraries, and their staff, were changed. The names given above are, it is hoped, ones by which the institutions concerned will be easily recognised.

The Author gratefully acknowledges the help and information which he has received from various sources. He wishes to place on record his thanks to: Miss M. Allum, National Army Museum; Mr J. Barber, Plymouth City Museum; Mr O. A. Baker, Plymouth Local History Library; Miss J. Bell, Totnes Museum; Miss T. Brown; Mrs G. Buckland, Royal Photographic Society; Mr V. Bonham-Carter, Exmoor Society; Lt. Commander K. V. Burns, Plymouth Local History Library; Mr B. T. Carter, National Maritime Museum; Mr R. E. Child, Rougemont House Museum, Exeter; Mr A. R. H. Cluer; Mrs S. G. Crowther; Mr R. Desmond, India Office Library; Mr M. Dowdle, Torquay Central Library; Mr J. Dyke, Lundy Museum; Mrs M. D. Evison, Budleigh Salterton Museum; Mr K. Fordyce, Torbay Aircraft Museum; Miss J. Gawne, Budleigh Salterton Museum; Mr C. W. Gott; Mr B. Greenhill C.M.G., Director, National Maritime Museum; The Misses E. Hamblin, Torquay Natural History Society Museum; Miss L. Hall, Dawlish Library; Mr W. Best Harris, City Librarian, Plymouth; Dr N. Harris, Curator, Torquay Natural History Society Museum; Mr S. Hiscock; Mr K. Hunt, Devon County Library; Mr S. Hunt, Royal Albert Memorial Museum, Exeter; Mr B. D. Hughes, Northam; Mr D. Hughes, Torrington; Mr A. Jewell, Keeper, Museum of English Rural Life; Mr P. A. Kennedy, County Archivist, Devon Record Office; Mrs C. Kinsman, Tavistock Library; Mr J. Lane, Beaford Centre; Mr J. Lomas; Mr J. E. Longhurst, Ilfracombe Museum; Mr R. M. Marks; Mr G. A. Morris, Curator, North Devon Athenaeum; Mr R. H. Nancekivell; Mr J. B. Nash, Torrington; Mrs M. A. Nash, Okehampton; Mr J. Newman, National Trust; Mr E. Ostroff, Smithsonian Institution, Washington D.C.; Miss J. E. Pauley; Mr J. Pedder; Mr J. R. Pike, Area Librarian, Torquay Central Library; Mr F. E. Pine, Plymouth General Hospital; Mr B. Pollard; Mr J. I. Ravilious, Beaford Centre; Mr C. H. Rock, Brixham Museum; Mrs M. M. Rowe, Exeter Record Office; Lady S. Sayer; Miss J. Sinclair, Holsworthy Library; Mr J. E. Stacey; Major N. K. Swaine, South Molton Museum; Dr D. B. Thomas, Science Museum; Mrs G. Vicarage, Sidmouth Museum; Mr J. P. Ward, Science Museum; Miss P. Waterer, North Devon College Library; Mr R. B. Wright. Above all the Author thanks his wife, Mary. If errors remain he himself is responsible; any positive mistakes which may be reported will be acknowledged and, if possible, corrected.

INTRODUCTION

4   The Royal William Victualling Yard at Stonehouse, Plymouth, as seen from the vicinity of Mount Edgcumbe House. The foreground, now part of Cornwall, was in fact administered by Devon till 1844. No doubt, in earlier times, it was thought wise to have a unified control over this waterway and its associated harbours. Calotype: W. H. Fox Talbot, 1845

The selection of photographs which forms the body of this book covers the period from 1845 to the outbreak of war in 1914. Queen Victoria came to the throne in 1837, the development of the Calotype process which took place in the early years of her reign being patented by W. H. Fox Talbot in 1841. At that time Devon, with the exception of the Plymouth area and the copper mining industry, was declining in relation to England as a whole. In terms of population the county had dwindled steadily from the position it once held as second or third in the order of English counties. Nevertheless, the Napoleonic Wars, and the presence of the fleet in Torbay, led to the growth of seaside resorts. Devon's scenery, as depicted by engravings and lithographs in books for the drawing room, encouraged the vogue which was to culminate in mass-tourism. Powerful assistance was given to this trend by the railways, increasing leisure, photography, and at the end of the period, by the picture postcard. Only Plymouth developed on a scale similar to that experienced elsewhere; a development which originated in the decision to construct the naval base at Dock to meet the widening demands of strategy in the time of William III. It seems appropriate, therefore, that the calotypes of the Royal William Victualling Yard at Stonehouse, Plymouth, made apparently by W. H. Fox Talbot, and those made about a decade later at Dock (Devonport) by L. Tripe – among the first photographic representations of Devonian subjects – present almost archetypal images of England's sea-power, vested, for the nation, in Devon.

The location of the county in the south-west of the British Isles has been an important determinant both of its historic role, and its mild climate. Compared to the average English county Devon is unusually large and it is one of the few having both a south and a north coast. Furthermore, these coasts and their hinterlands are of a different character: the north has grand cliff scenery and comes under the bracing influence of Atlantic winds; whilst within the more equable south are situated the fine natural harbours from which Armadas, ancient and modern, have set sail. Inland, the country is extremely hilly; through it rises the massif of Dartmoor, a domain set apart by geological structure from the rest of the county. The presence of this highland area, and the Devon part of Exmoor, have a pronounced influence on the climate, the rainfall and the severity of the winters on and around the moors being in marked contrast to that of the coastal valleys not far away.

Variations of climate, landscape, and soil have moulded the Devonian characteristics, human and architectural alike. There has been on one hand the pervasive influence of the sea, and on the other the beauty of stream, woodland, and moorland, soils of varying fertility, and mineral wealth. From the sea was born a long history of adventurous seamanship and exploration: from soil and western rain, dairy farming, clotted cream, and the once renowned orchards which in the early eighteenth century produced much cider for the London market. From differences in geology are derived the long, low, granite farms of Dartmoor; the stone and slate bartons of Hartland and Mortehoe; and the cob and thatch of central, south and east Devon. These features attracted the early photographers. The two themes "Land and Sea" run through Devon's history and find an echo in many Devonian families which, like the writer's, have kept one foot on deck, one hand on the plough.

Devon's prosperity in earlier times had been based on a four-fold economy of a woollen industry, mining, fishing, and of course agriculture. Devon serge had been the most important English export at the beginning of the eighteenth century; but competition from other parts of the country, and the Napoleonic Wars, brought the industry to an end just before the Victorian period. The once thriving mining industry had almost ceased to exist in the eighteenth century. Even so, the Devon Great Consuls Mine, opened in 1844, and reaching peak output of copper in 1862, was of world-wide importance, but mining then became only a minor contributor to Devon's wealth. There was a similar decline in the fishing industry. In the late sixteenth century the fishing grounds

5   The fleet anchored in the roadstead known as the Hamoaze situated near the mouth of the river Tamar. The fourth ship from the left is thought to be the *Conqueror*, launched at Devonport in 1855 and wrecked in the West Indies in 1861. The proximity of Plymouth to England's old rivals France and Spain, contributed to her importance during and after mediaeval times. *c.* 1859

had been extended across the Atlantic, and the enterprise of the Devon ports dominated the trade during the seventeenth century. Fishing was still a major occupation during the nineteenth century and only during the first decade of the twentieth century did the shoals begin to desert some of the inshore grounds. It will be obvious that of the four traditional occupations only farming and fishing were of significance in 1914, and fishing failed to survive the First World War. Devon had seen better times.

The seventeenth and eighteenth centuries had been prosperous ones for Devon agriculture and the county had the reputation of being well farmed. But the agricultural interest suffered severely from the slump which followed the end of the Napoleonic Wars, a period which saw much rural emigration to the cities. In the 1840s opportunities in the New World, and in particular the gold of California, exercised a powerful attraction to the rural labourer and the advertisements of emigrant ships became a prominent feature in the local press. James Caird, writing in 1851, complains that "the rent of land in Devon has increased by a third in the last 20 years" and he states that farmers are saying that "rents must be reduced, or prices rise". The small inland towns reached their maximum population about this time and thenceforward declined when the railways offered cheap and easy transport. By the end of the 1870s Devon was involved in the great agricultural slump which lasted for the remainder of the period. H. Rider Haggard wrote a very pessimistic review of Devon farming in 1902. Farm wages in general were low. A vigorous class of tenant farmers survived, but for the labourer conditions compared unfavourably with those in other counties.

The nineteenth century was a period of transition for the people of Devon, as indeed it was for the nation as a whole. A dwindling population in the countryside, and in the small towns and villages which had once been flourishing centres of the cloth industry, and the absence or small scale of urban growth, were part of the price paid by Devon for being spared the worst aspects of contemporary urban growth and industrial development. But the county was not spared its share of social problems. A thousand people died of cholera at Plymouth in 1849; likewise the county capital, Exeter, experienced dirt, disease, and overcrowding which, though on a relatively minor scale, were as bad as conditions given greater prominence in government Blue Books. Exeter, at the end of the nineteenth century, has been described as a social and cultural survival from pre-industrial England.

If the advent of the railways assisted emigration it also facilitated the growth of a major new industry – the tourist trade. By the end of the century tourism was making an important contribution to the economy of the county. Exmouth and Teignmouth had already become resorts in the eighteenth century. The closure of the Continent by the Napoleonic Wars had increased the flow of discerning visitors to both south and north Devon in the early years of the nineteenth century; but it was not till the railways reached Exeter in 1844, Torquay and Plymouth in 1848, and Barnstaple in 1854, that the means were available for a wider spectrum of the population to visit the county. The first excursion train to Exeter from Birmingham ran in 1850. By 1914 the holiday trade, with its supporting services, was on the way to becoming second only to agriculture in importance and the historic industries had shrunk, or were shrinking, to a point where they were insignificant. Without any doubt the coming of the railways was the most important event in the fortunes of Devon in Victorian times. Once communications had been improved in this way a certain physical and social isolation was at an end. Former fishing villages such as Ilfracombe, Lynmouth, Budleigh Salterton, Dawlish and Paignton, were stimulated to develop as resorts, and it was through the railways that Devon came to share the new engineering skills with the rest of the nation. In tackling the obstacle posed by the river Tamar, I. K. Brunel gave Devon and Cornwall one of the most original structures of the age in the form of the Royal Albert Bridge. Early rail visitors came to a county that was unspoilt; both wild Dartmoor and the Devon part of Exmoor were far more extensive then than they are today.

As one would expect, photographs of Devon from the period up to 1880, by which date 'instantaneous' photography had become possible, are not numerous, and those that have survived are frequently found to be in a poor state of preservation. After this date there is an increasing supply of material, but, as in any field, masterpieces are few. It has been a pleasure to discover, during the course of the searches on which the selection in this book is based, that five Devonians: R. Burnard, W. J. Chapman, A. W. Searley, J. Stabb, and L. Tripe, all produced work which helps to form a rich source of visual material concerned with Devon, her people, and their occupations. One would not claim that any of them, with the possible exception of Linnaeus Tripe, are very important above a regional level, but they did each have an eye for a telling subject, and the photographic record of Devon would be much poorer without their work. (Some biographical notes on these photographers are given below).

The long reign of Victoria ended, neatly, at the turn of the century, as if destiny were saying 'now there will be a complete break'. Generally speaking there had been stability and prosperity which was not affected by minor wars, or even by the Crimea or South Africa, but a break it was not to be. To one writing in August 1974, the sixtieth anniversary of the fateful summer of 1914, when the comparative peace, tranquillity and community life, illustrated by the photographs, were transformed by the tumultuous events and ever-recurring crises of the present century, the Edwardian decade appears to have been the real end of the era – so great were the changes which subsequently occurred.

Devon is one of the longest-inhabited parts of the British Isles, if not the longest.

The Palaeolithic families who, in the far distant past, came to the red soils and limestone caves of what we now call Torbay, discovered a territory of embowered hills rising to distant blue, granitic heights. Even today, in this nuclear age, the broad green land of Devon under its vast skies, arching across the county from sea to sea, seems too inscrutable to be troubled by the ephemeral activities of mankind. The modern traveller may feel, as his Victorian forbears felt, that even when Lundy is taking the full force of an Atlantic gale, and the storm spray is drenching Hartland and Start Point, benevolence broods over the farms, hamlets and harbours, cradled in the Devonshire hills.

6 The ports of both south and north Devon played a part in the populating of North America especially during the middle decades of the nineteenth century. Many ships bringing timber to the British Isles carried emigrants on their return voyages. One such ship, the *Margaret*, dries out her sails in Torquay harbour. *c.* 1855

Notes on some photographers active in Devon 1845-1914

No attempt is made to describe local photographers many of whom are represented by photographs in the selection. The following are either Devonian photographers who produced work of a regional importance, or photographers of national importance who came to Devon and did photographic work here.

Bedford, Francis. *b.* 1816, *d.* 1894. Topographic photographer, traveller in the Near East. Produced a series of stereoscopic slides "Devonshire Illustrated", and "Ten Photographic Views of Exeter", and individual photographs. Visited Ilfracombe in the early 1860s. (Example, Plate 139.)

Burnard, Robert, F.S.A. *b.* Plymouth 1848, *d.* Stokeinteignhead 1920. Successful businessman in family firm at Plymouth, early photographer of Dartmoor. Became interested in archaeology in the 1870s at which time his father bought a house near Dartmeet. From 1888–1908 one of the most active archaeologists and recorders of Dartmoor, he used his camera to make a comprehensive and fully-documented survey of the moor. (Examples, Plates 9, 50, 106, 108, 111, 120.)

Chapman, W. J. *b.* Exeter 1830, *d.* 1923. Founder of the photographic firm of Chapman & Sons which opened at Dawlish in 1863, and, involving four generations of the family, operated for over 100 years. Early in the present century the firm started to produce postcards of Devon, including Dartmoor; coverage of the Dawlish district was very thorough. The Chapman family has lodged a representative collection of annotated photographs at the Dawlish Public Library. (Examples, Plates 74, 75, 81, 104, 109.)

Fox Talbot, William Henry. *b.* Melbury 1800, *d.* Lacock 1877. Scientist, author, traveller, and inventor of the calotype. It has been assumed that it was whilst staying at Mount Edgcumbe, till 1844 a part of the county of Devon, that Fox Talbot made the calotypes of the house, and the views of the Royal William Victualling Yard, Stonehouse (Plymouth), taken from its vicinity, which are ascribed to him. However, until the results of research now in progress becomes available, it would be unwise to regard this as certainty for it is known that Fox Talbot, secretive in some ways, did make his processes known to a few close friends and it is not impossible that the negatives were made by one of them. Other Devon calotypes ascribed to Fox Talbot, but not reproduced here, show Ugbrooke House, and Chudleigh Rocks. (Example, Plate 4.)

Frith, Francis. *b.* Chesterfield 1822, *d.* Cannes 1898. Apprentice, wholesale grocer, prolific topographic photographer, traveller in the Near East; founder of Frith & Co. of Reigate, eventually the world's largest photographic publishers. Though the work of F. Frith has received detailed study elsewhere it would be unthinkable not to mention him in these notes as more plates in this selection derive from the work of his firm than from any other source. As none of these photographs have been positively identified as the personal work of Francis Frith they have all been attributed to the company. Frith photographs are widely distributed in museums and libraries in Devon and these sources are credited in this book. One photograph however has come direct from the "Rothman Collection of Photographs by F. Frith" which now owns and conserves the original material. Much of the Frith work on Devon was of a purely topographic type, but at the same time many examples successfully combine localities with pleasing groups of human figures. The fact that the photographs were systematically indexed adds to their documentary value. (Examples, Plates 8, 13, 29, 64, 65, 66, 67, 68, 69, 83, 110, 138, 141, 143, 145, 151, 153.)

Martin, Paul. *b.* France 1864, *d.* London 1944. French engraver and photographer who spent almost all his life in England. He took a holiday at Ilfracombe in 1891, and again in 1894. Though doubtless he made many photographs during these visits only a few have been located during the search for material for this collection. (Example, Plate 131.)

Searley, Albert William, F.R.Hist.Soc. *b.* Exeter 1860, *d.* Kingkerswell 1942. From 1884, headmaster of Kingkerswell village school, *c.* 1902 joined the staff of Devon County Council, later became supervisor of manual instruction in secondary schools throughout the county. Travelled in Europe. He designed work in wood and stone; made a large collection of slides of Devon subjects. (Examples, Plates 28, 42, 51, 72, 80, 84, 87, 88, 89, 112.)

Stabb, John. *b.* 1865, *d.* Torquay 1917. A noted Devon ecclesiologist, described 264 of the county's churches and illustrated them photographically. At one time lived in London where he was involved in professional photography. (Examples, Plates 34, 61, 100, 102, 105, 132, 149.)

Tripe, Linnaeus. *b.* Devonport 1822, *d.* Devonport 1902. Captain 51st Madras Native Infantry; later Honorary Major-General. Government photographer in Burma 1855 and Madras 1856–60. (Examples, Plates 2, 3.)

THE DEVON SCENE

7 A Devon thatcher. One of the creators of the varied forms which cover the traditional Devon cottage; he is wearing protective clothing in the form of leather knee-pads, and a shield to protect his right hand when pushing in the hazel "spears" by which the thatch is secured. 1902

8 *Above* The Square, Inner Hope. Devon cottages as they had been for centuries; this was an essentially functional architecture employing local materials. Apart from the loss of the thatch on the extreme right, and the addition of television aerials, the scene is little different today. Photograph: F. Frith & Co., 1904

9 *Below* Stone, clay, straw, and wood were the rural building materials in Devon; they were available in almost all parts of the county and the constructional methods employed were such that any industrious man could lend a hand with building. This photograph was taken at Samford Courtenay. The cob wall of the barn on the left of centre, is suffering because the thatch has not been maintained in good condition. Photograph: Robert Burnard; August, 1890

THE CITIES

Exeter

10 The arch erected by the Decoration Committee at the top of Fore Street for the Devon County
Agricultural Show. The geographical position of Exeter had given the city the air and status of a provincial
capital. Stimulated by the railways, the Royal Agricultural Show had been held there as early as 1850.
Photograph: J. F. Long; May, 1894

11   The west façade of Exeter Cathedral, mother church of the South West as it was during the proclamation of the accession of King Edward VII. Photograph: Heath & Bradnee; January, 1901

12   The annual visit of the City Fathers to the entrance of the canal at Turf. The development of Exeter as a port had been frustrated since the thirteenth century, when the Countess of Devon had a weir built across the Exe two miles below the city. It was three hundred years before the obstruction was successfully by-passed by the canal. Photograph: 1886

13 The High Street, a mixture of mediaeval, Georgian, and Victorian buildings, with, on the left, the arcade of the Guildhall built on to an earlier structure in 1592. Photograph: F. Frith & Co., 1905

14 The Exeter School of Art was founded in 1854 and was inspired by Sir Stafford Northcote. After the death of Albert, Prince Consort, Exeter combined art, science, and museum resources as a memorial to him. The gentleman on the left is the art master, the occasion being the Spring Exhibition, 1857

Plymouth

15 *Top* The Citadel from Mount Batten. One of the few English forts to survive from the seventeenth century; some of the ramparts are 60′ high and 20′ thick. On the south side, seen here, the ground falls steeply from the upper battery to the lower, situated on the rocks, and the complicated system of bastions on the landward side – some say they were built to keep Plymouth itself in order – was unnecessary. These lower outworks, visible in the photograph, were demolished in 1888.

16 *Above* The Barbican, evidently an outpost of the castle, stood here in former times. The quay and its adjacent buildings were an essentially Elizabethan extension of Plymouth. The buildings are warehouses, a lodging house, a ship's chandler, and a public house. Bricks and casks are stacked on the quay. This is reputed to be the earliest known photograph of the Barbican. *c.* 1865

17 *Above* Children's Corner,
Plymouth Hoe, *c.* 1900
18 *Right* The fourth prize to the fore
as a Horse Parade proceeds from
Stonehouse to Plymouth along Union
Street which, linking the two towns,
is an example of the town planning
ideas of the Plymouth architect,
Foulston. The occasion was August
Bank Holiday, 1896

19 These community buildings were devastated by enemy action in World War II; St. Andrew's Church and the Guildhall behind it have been restored, the area on the right occupied by the Civic Offices, and narrow Basket Street together with St. Andrew's Cross, is completely changed. "No British municipality can boast of finer or more commodious offices", stated the *Western Daily Mercury* on the opening of the Civic Offices in 1873.

20 The fleet in Plymouth Sound: the *German* Fleet, eight battleships and seven cruisers; never before had Plymouth seen such a large fleet of foreign warships. The *Western Morning News* stated that their proprietors "feel convinced that the interests of both countries are best served by a mutual good understanding, by the maintenance of peaceful relations, and by the recognition of the fact that the field of industry throughout the world is so extensive that there is no cause for other than friendly rivalry". Photograph: J. Valentine; July 1904

21 A Plymouth and Devonport horse bus turns into Bedford Street from Old Town Street. Beyond St. Andrew's churchyard on the left is the site on which the Civic Offices were built in 1873 (see photograph 19). *c.* 1868

22 From this mercantile quay at the Barbican, Sutton Harbour, Plymouth, countless explorers, adventurers and voyagers have embarked over the centuries, but, in the hearts of the English-speaking peoples of both sides of the Atlantic, none of them eclipse the fame of the Pilgrim Fathers, who, having called at Plymouth for repairs, finally set sail for the New World on 6 September, 1620. Here is the scene as the Edwardians knew it near what are now called the Mayflower Steps. *c.* 1910

23 *Above* Troops fire a *Feu-de-Joie* and a monster bonfire is ready for ignition in the evening. The place is Plymouth Hoe, and the occasion, Queen Victoria's Diamond Jubilee Celebrations, June, 1897

24 *Left* It was not until the completion of the mile-long breakwater in 1841 that Plymouth Sound was protected from southerly gales and became a really safe anchorage. In the photograph Mr Holderness of the Seamen's Mission has delivered a parcel of books and a few cheerful words to the lighthouse keepers on the breakwater.
Photograph: E. J. Jarvis; December, 1906

COMMUNITY LIFE

25   The porbeagle shark was trapped in a trammel-net, although but for the fact that it had swallowed part of a boat – the distension caused can be seen above the lateral gill-slits – it is unlikely that it would have been caught. It is thought that the young man in the straw hat was a visiting bank clerk; the rest of the group were inhabitants of Budleigh Salterton. Photograph: F. T. Blackburn; 1906

26   *Next page* Making a lobster pot at Budleigh Salterton. The man on the left is working on the flat base of a pot. On the right, the narrow entrance having been formed, the withes are being bent over as the first step in forming the outer wall of what is in fact more of a trap than a pot. c. 1895

27 Bideford collar factory girls with their steam irons; *c.* 1895

28 During the eighteenth century Tiverton had been the most highly industrial town in Devon. In 1816 John Heathcoat, driven from Loughborough by the machine-breaking Luddites, took over one of the last of the woollen mills and established the lace factory which has held an important place in the economy of the district ever since. Photograph: A. W. Searley; *c.* 1908

29 The making of Honiton lace was not confined to the town from which it derives its name. The industry had faltered after the introduction of machine-made net in the second decade of the nineteenth century, but royal patronage, including the christening robe which Queen Victoria ordered and which has been worn at royal christenings ever since, helped to keep the craft going. Beer, where this photograph was taken, had 400 workers in the 1850s, including, it is said, some of the best. In bad fishing seasons the lace makers of Beer earned more than the men. Photograph: F. Frith & Co; 1901

30 *Left* A detachment of the North Devon Hussars, with drawn swords, clatter through Northam. They had come from their annual camp at Westward Ho! *c.* 1895

31 *Left, below* The fire brigade had a difficult task when fire ravaged the centre of Ilfracombe at the height of the holiday season in 1896.

32 *Below* The Devon and Cornwall Homoeopathic and General Hospital moved to new premises in Lockyer Street, Plymouth, in 1895 and it seems probable that this photograph, of the operating theatre, was taken soon after. The anaesthetist holds an ether or chloroform inhaler over the patient's nose, the surgeon sits waiting by the window.

33 *Next page* Evidently some dissatisfaction was felt with the old lady's face for the one that appears in the photograph had been cut from another photograph and stuck on. The shop was situated in the village of Ashreigny; *c.* 1905

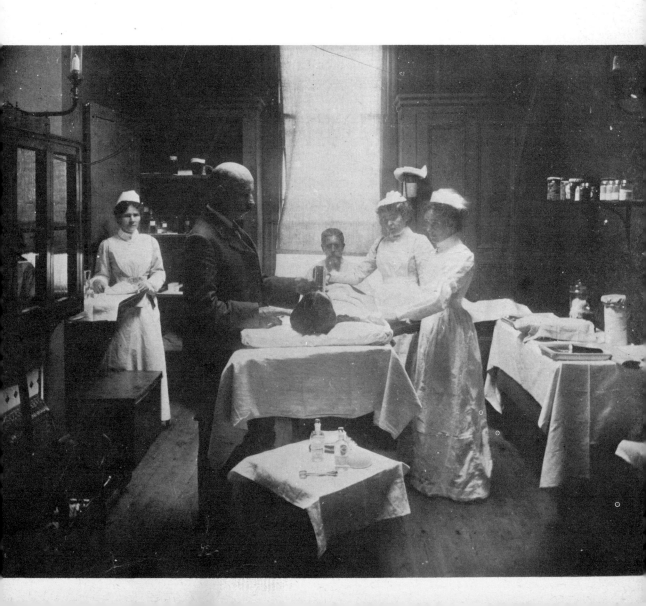

34 That the Maypole Dance was re-enacted in Victorian Devon is proved by the number of photographs of it which survive. These children at Kingkerswell are innocent enough, but in earlier centuries there had been efforts to suppress Maypole dancing in Devon. Photograph: J. Stabb; *c.* 1900

35 *Bottom* Fashionable gowns and millinery to attract the visitors at the well-appointed Stevens drapers shop in Ilfracombe High Street. *c.* 1895

36 A cyclists' rally on Bideford Quay: the couple seated on the tandem, near the centre of the group, had come in from Petticombe five miles away; at this date the bicycle was helping to break down social barriers. On the east bank of the river Torridge may be seen more extensive woodland than exists there today. *c.* 1890

37 The Burnard family at Huccaby House, Princetown; Robert Burnard, several of whose photographs are included in this collection, stands second from the right in the back row. He supports his granddaughter Sylvia, now Lady Sayer, whose work as a conservationist in our own time is well known. Photograph, 1909

38   A game of bowls behind one of the houses of the Strand, Bideford; *c*. 1890

Halsdon v. Dolton Cricket Match

39 *Top left* Hancock's Up-To-Date Switchback Railway at Torquay Regatta Fair; *c.* 1900

40 *Left* Meadfoot Beach, Torquay. Photograph: J. C. Dinham, 1907

41 *Above* The staff of Halsdon House and Dolton village cricket team sit down to tea after a cricket match; the car appears to be an early Rolls. *c.* 1912

42 A barrel organ player with his monkey at the amusement fair associated with Torquay Regatta. Photograph: A. W. Searley; *c.* 1905

43 *Top* The Scott family seen in the garden of their Little Torrington home. Photograph: W. J. Bell; *c.* 1895

44 Members of the Ancient Order of Foresters on parade at the small village of Black Torrington; May, 1908

45 Travelling people. The James Penfold wagon with its varied assortment of brushes, carpets, and oilcloths on Bideford Quay; *c.* 1888

GREAT EVENTS

46 "The Triple Entente Tea Powers": High Bickington. The house party at Kingsford Hill House, held in order to raise money to build a Village Hall, went on as planned in spite of external events. It was August 1914; a war that was to change the course of western civilisation, and in particular the status of Great Britain, had started

47 *Below* The Royal Albert Bridge over the river Tamar during its construction; the last engineering work made to the designs of I. K. Brunel and one of the world's most interesting bridges. The timber in the foreground is part of the supporting structure used in the construction of the spans on the Devon side. These spans, consisting of elliptical tubes $16\frac{3}{4}'$ wide and with a curved length of 460', were floated out, and, as the tide went down rested on the piers. The towers were built up and allowed to set under the spans, as they were jacked up, three feet at a time; 1859

48 *Right* The Great Gale. Ships' crews thought that they were safe in Brixham's outer harbour, well-protected on all quarters except north, but the wind changed direction during the night. Forty vessels were wrecked and at least 100 lives lost; January, 1866

49 *Below right* Celebration of the Jubilee of Queen Victoria at Torquay. After thanksgiving services in all the churches, a Royal Salute was fired from the pier. Then representatives of all the trades and public services paraded in order to testify to Torquay's loyalty. In the foreground are the Yeoman Cavalry, and in the distance the lifeboat, drawn by horses. June, 1887

50 The Great Blizzard: The Princetown-Plymouth Train. The lady passengers naturally became alarmed when the engine driver said "We ought never to have started" (*The Blizzard in the West*). They spent 36 hours in the train before making their way to a Dartmoor farm. By then carriages, with closed doors, were full of snow up to the hat racks and the train had almost been buried, such was the ferocity of the hurricane. Photograph: Robert Burnard; March, 1891

51 The Great Blizzard: Fore Street, Kingsbridge. The town underwent "some wretched experiences" during "the gravest atmospheric disturbance of the century – in this part of the world at all events" (*The Blizzard in the West*). Several commercial travellers who arrived in the town on the Monday were compelled to remain till Friday, when they escaped from confinement by going to Plymouth – by steamer. Photograph: A. W. Searley; March 1891

53 *Right* Unveiling of a Boer War Memorial Tablet at South Molton. Whatever the rest of the country thought of him, General Sir Redvers Buller, V.C., commander of British forces in South Africa, was immensely popular in his own county. This was the scene as he unveiled a tablet to commemorate the loyal and distinguished services rendered by the 23 local men who had served in the campaign. Photograph: Elizabeth Askew; April, 1903

52 Celebration of the Queen's Diamond Jubilee at Budleigh Salterton. "An occasion of public rejoicing affords a good test of the feeling which animates a village community. It gives an opportunity of shewing whether, and how far, people are willing to work together to arrange a holiday for the common enjoyment of all, and it gives an opportunity also for shewing with what amount of orderliness and good sense people can spend a holiday." (*East Budleigh and Budleigh Salterton Parish Magazine*). June, 1897

54 *Right* A celebration, thought to be on the Relief of Mafeking, at Bradworthy. In no part of the country was news of the welcome relief received with greater enthusiasm than in Devon, where the operations had a peculiar interest as many Devonians were involved in the fighting. Six of the girls in the photograph appear, enigmatically, to be holding cords

55 *Left* There were two General Elections in 1910. In the South Molton Division, Liberal George Lambert, who, as he stated in an election notice "had volunteered for active service in any part of the world, and whose Militia Regiment was the first ordered to leave England" defeated his Unionist opponent Colonel Perowne in both campaigns. Photograph: Elizabeth Askew; 1910

56 *Below* Mounted supporters rode into Holsworthy Square brandishing their spears to celebrate the election of John Spear, Liberal Unionist candidate for the Tavistock Division; December, 1910

57 Dartmouth, the Butterwalk, a group of four houses completed in 1640 at the height of the town's prosperity resulting from the Newfoundland cod trade. The building is considered to be the best surviving example of the seventeenth-century Devonian style in domestic architecture. Damaged by enemy action in 1943, it is now restored. The colonnade was used as a butter market between the years 1780-1828. Photograph, *c.* 1870

58 North Quay, Torquay. The nearest ship is the *Emily* of Torquay and Teignmouth. On the extreme left is the Torbay Hotel, which had been built in the early 1850s. Photograph, *c.* 1875

59 *Below* Totnes. Arcades and slate-hung façades are typical of the ancient town. Seen here is the High Street with the east gate, near which stands a knife-grinder. The arcaded Church Walk, on the left, was taken down in 1878 to provide a view of St. Mary's parish church which had been renovated in 1862. Photograph, *c.* 1875

60 Torquay from Vane Hill before the building of the outer harbour in 1890. Waldon Hill dominates the centre of the photograph and to its right is Fleet Street running up the valley in which the shopping centre of modern Torquay is situated. Torbay Road, running round the base of Waldon Hill, had been constructed in the 1840s. Almost all the development shown in the photograph is of nineteenth century origin. Photograph, *c.* 1880

61 *Below* Torquay, the Ladies' Bathing Cove, one of the many small beaches found along the limestone and permian cliffs of this varied coast. The life-boat station had been established in 1876, being the gift of Mrs Mary Brundet of Manchester. Photograph: J. Stabb, 1886

62 *Top* Babbacombe, a family group on the lawn of the Cary Arms; on the terrace the nurse holds the baby. About 15 years after this photograph was taken, fire broke out at the *Glen*, the cottage with three first-floor windows at the centre of this scene, and Miss Emma Keynes was found murdered. Her footman, who was later found guilty, became famous as *the man they could not hang*. Photograph, *c.* 1870
63 The Garden Room at the *Glen*, Babbacombe. *c.* 1880

64 *Top* Paignton Harbour. Like many seaside villages in Devon, Paignton expanded when the railway reached it in 1859. Photograph: F. Frith & Co., 1912

65 Newton Abbot. The locals pause in Courtenay Street for the Frith cameraman; Thomas and Sons' bread van advertises steam ovens and malt bread. In the distance the remaining tower of St Leonard's, which, as the inscription records, had been given two new bells in 1887 ''to the glory of God and as a memorial of the Jubilee of Queen Victoria's accession to the throne''. Photograph: F. Frith & Co., 1895

66 *Top left* Sidmouth, Fore Street.
The railway had reached Sidmouth in
1874, the first cars were on the roads
when this photograph was taken, but as
elsewhere in Devon the stage coach was
still the means of reaching outlying
places and remained so for many years.
Photograph: F. Frith & Co., 1903

67 *Above* Beer, a fishing village, and at
one time a pillow-lace and smuggling
centre. The thatch and cobbles of
Fore Street have been replaced, but
the little stream still flows through the
conduit with the unusual coping
stone. Photograph: F. Frith & Co.,
1901

68 *Left* Teignmouth Beach. Beyond
the pier the entrance to the harbour is
situated; from it china clay was
exported in the nineteenth century as
is the case today. Photograph:
F. Frith & Co., 1891

69 Honiton, New Street. On the road from Exeter to London, Honiton was noted for its fine pillow-lace (see photograph No 29). Photograph: F. Frith & Co., 1903

THE LAND

70 Puslinch. A wood-cutter at the porch of his south Devon cottage. The hard bowler hat was generally worn at the time and afforded more protection from knocks than the felt hat or cap which succeeded it; it was to all intents a crash-helmet. Note the locally-made jug and the polypody fern growing in the masonry. *c.* 1890

71 Ashreigny. Though the number of sheep bred in Devon declined slightly in Victorian times, mutton and wool continued to be one of the mainstays of the county's agriculture. Here we see the Squire family displaying their sheep at Furze Barton. On the extreme left is the ram, and in the right hand corner a shepherd holds a ewe in a position convenient for shearing its fleece. *c.* 1900

72 *Right* Kingsbridge, a thriving place in the nineteenth century. This languid bull is seen in the town's important cattle market, whose history goes back to the thirteenth century. Photograph: A. W. Searley; *c.* 1895

73 Salcombe Regis. A South Devon farmer, Mr Russell, stands with his three daughters by his first wife; he rests his hand on the shoulder of his second wife. *c.* 1885

74 At Bampton one of the main markets for the wild Exmoor ponies is held each October; by this month the foals are ready to be taken from the mares. One of the distinguishing features of the breed is the mealy colour of the muzzles, visible, on some of these ponies which have been rounded up, and labelled, prior to being driven in to the Fair. Photograph: Chapman & Son, 1912

75 *Top* Princetown. Prisoners at Dartmoor Prison were able to work on the 2,000 acre prison farm. "It provided a healthy out-door activity and enabled them to acquire knowledge and skill which they might put to use on release. But the work of making the Dartmoor subsoil fertile was so heavy, and the labour so plentiful, that the methods were not applicable other than to a prison farm." (*H. Rider Haggard*). Photograph: Chapman & Son, 1908

76 Ilfracombe district. Some scything is still necessary inside the gate and in odd corners, but the McCormick reaper-binder, which had transformed harvesting in the American mid-west, made its appearance in Devon late in the nineteenth century and the basic design of it remained unchanged till the arrival of the combine-harvesters in the late 1940s. *c.* 1895

77 Dolton. A common scene in every Devon village in Victorian and Edwardian times. In the latter half of the twentieth century it is more convenient for the motorised farrier to visit the horses. Photographed by a Russian student; *c*. 1913

78 *Top* Lustleigh. "A woman on a tedding machine naturally attracted great attention. She is an enthusiastic practical farmer who has studied farming in many counties" (*The Daily Graphic*). The slightly comical action of this type of tedding machine earned it the name *donkey-kicker*; in the photograph one leg has just kicked! August, 1907

79 Hatherleigh, where in 1830 there had been riotous attempts to break up threshing machines. A pause, at Passaford, to fill the tank of the traction engine and stand for the photographer. Few farms employed as many as ten men and for big operations neighbours co-operated. Empty sacks are positioned to collect the grain on the lower part of the thresher; one full sack is held by the farmer. 1910

80 Newton Abbot. Farmers' wives made butter by taking Devonshire clotted cream and simply stirring and beating it with their hands. Here the process is taking place in the kitchen at Bradley Mill; the stone floor is unusually irregular but the range is typical of the period. Photograph: A. W. Searley, *c.* 1900

81 Lydford. To make real Devonshire cream, take the rich milk of Devon cows. Stand it in a pan in the cool for a day, then carefully place the pan over a gentle heat until the cream begins to crinkle. Allow it to cool slowly, and then use a skimmer to lift off the cream. Photograph: Chapman & Son, 1912

82 South Molton: farm education; a class in progress in part of the South Molton market buildings. The girls are receiving instruction in butter making. First of all the separator on the left would have been used, then the churns – the process was essentially one of squeezing the water and butter-milk from the fatty solids. 1892

83 Bideford Market. Most of the Devon markets were concerned mainly with farm produce and livestock, the two being held as separate events, if not on separate days. Fruit and vegetables, in baskets still called *panniers*, are seen on the left, whilst boots and shoes, and some local pottery, are displayed on the right. Photograph: F. Frith & Co., 1907

84 *Below* Otter Hunting; a kill. No doubt the hunt was enjoyed for its own sake and arguments as to whether hunting, trapping, or poisoning was the most humane method of controlling the otter population exercised the minds of those concerned very little. Photograph: A. W. Searley

85 Jack Russell, huntsman and founder of the *Jack Russell* breed of terrier. He also found time to be vicar of Swimbridge. *c.* 1880

THE SEA

86 Messing around with boats, at an early age, at Appledore. All three boys, members of the Slade family, are said to have become successful ships' masters or owners

87 *Left* Shipbuilding was carried on at almost all the ports and harbours of the county. Brixham, where this photograph was taken, had five yards at the close of the nineteenth century. Photograph: A. W. Searley, *c.* 1895

88 *Below* Combined operations at the small fishing village of Hallsands. A lighthouse was first established at Start Point which forms the background, in 1836. Photograph: A. W. Searley, *c.* 1900

89 *Top* Shipbuilding and fishing. The whole economy of Brixham was based on shipbuilding, fishing, and supporting trades and crafts. In the 1840s there were 270 vessels in the port. By 1890 the number stood just under 300; almost all of them were owned by their skippers. Photograph: A. W. Searley, *c.* 1900
90 The fishing industry. Throughout the nineteenth century fishing was an important Devon occupation. Plymouth overtook Brixham as the foremost fishing port in the 1870s. Fish were marketed at various places in Plymouth till, in 1892, the Barbican market shown here was opened. Catches were likely to have included herring, sole, whiting, plaice and mackerel. *c.* 1900

91   Seamanship. Learning to scull in the inner harbour at Brixham. Photograph: S. C. Fox (Cardiff)

92   *Below* Towing to sea in the Taw-Torridge estuary. A schooner and two ketches are being towed out over Bideford Bar where there is almost always a breeze. In south Devon, too, sailing ships were towed out of harbour during this period. Photograph: S. C. Fox (Cardiff)

93 *Top* Barking canvas, one of the supporting activities carried on at the fishing villages. A mainsail and staysail have been treated and hang drying at one of the three Brixham barking yards. The jibs and topsail are being brushed with barking solution, the exact recipe of which was a closely kept secret. *c.* 1900

94 The lifeboat is launched into a choppy sea at Sidmouth

95 A group of herring fishermen at Clovelly. The men wearing the Tam-o-Shanters also manned the lifeboat. Herrings were the most important catch off the north Devon coast but have, at various times, disappeared from the fishing grounds.
Photograph: J. Valentine, *c.* 1885

96 Construction of what were, at the time, the largest docks ever built simultaneously, was completed for the Royal Navy at Devonport in 1907. Several dry docks and a basin, in all 120 acres, were excavated and the retaining walls built in concrete and faced with limestone. The photograph shows No 9 dock under construction. 1899

97 In 1863 *H.M.S Britannia the 4th* arrived in the Dart to act as a training ship for Royal Navy cadets. Dartmouth was chosen because of its stretches of protected river water, easy shore access, and playing fields. The *Britannia* was joined by the *Hindustan*, on the left, and the original *Britannia* was replaced by the fifth ship of that name in 1869. Over 300 cadets occupied the floating school at one time, but it was realised as early as 1874 that the health and development of young cadets must suffer through living on a ship. Photograph: *Torquay Times*, c. 1900

98 A trawler ketch, running before the wind, off Brixham

99 Dartmouth Royal Regatta, showing the waterfront before the Boatfloat and the New Embankment were constructed in 1890. On the foreground jetty is the terminal broad gauge track of the South Devon Railway; to the right of it lies the steam paddle-boat *Pilot*. 1865

100 *Top* Visitors disembarking at Ilfracombe from the paddle steamer *Britannia*. Most Bristol Channel ports were served by pleasure steamers during this period. Photograph: J. Stabb, *c.* 1897

101 The steamer pier at Ilfracombe, where vessels can lie afloat at all states of the tide, was built by the town in 1871. In plan it formed a loop and on the rock at the centre of this loop there formerly stood the warp-house; by means of the capstan set up there sailing ships were assisted in and out of harbour. The steamer nearest the camera is the *Earl of Dunraven. c.* 1895

102 It was not always possible to disembark on a quay or pier; on some steep beaches it was the practice to run the bow into the shingle and to bring a gangway into use. In this photograph of Clovelly beach, visitors are being ferried ashore. Photograph: J. Stabb

103 Almost all Devon estuaries had ferry services. Shown here are two visiting ladies making the crossing from Instow to Appledore on the river Torridge. The sheet is made fast – not generally to be recommended on the Taw-Torridge estuary. Photograph: S. C. Fox (Cardiff), *c.* 1906

104 The Druid's Arms, Drewsteignton, on the edge of the moor, is twelve miles, as the crow flies, from Exeter; it was longer, and presented some stiff climbs, for the brake. Photograph: Chapman & Son, *c.* 1905

105 Beardown. The building is probably just a small farm shelter, but the form of construction suggests the survival, till the late nineteenth century, of the methods used in the Bronze Age dwellings of Grimspound and other early Dartmoor settlements. The thatch appears to have some heather in it, and the ridge consists of peat *vags*. Photograph: J. Stabb, 1886
106 *Right* The Misses Coaker. Photograph: R. Burnard; September, 1892

107 *Above* Walking through the
bracket. Photograph: Edward
Pocknell; *c.* 1910

108 *Right* In mediaeval times tin was
obtained on Dartmoor by *streaming*;
then surface working became the rule;
finally it had to be mined. The granite
had to be broken down in order to
release the ore. The big water wheel
at Whiteworks supplied the power for
the *stamps* seen on its right.
Photograph: R. Burnard; June, 1889

109 *Above right* A cast-iron range,
an open fire, and a small bread oven
are all fitted into a large open hearth
of an early date. The open fire is
prepared for lighting with wood, but
peat *vags* would certainly be the basic
fuel in both fire and range.
Photograph: Chapman & Son; 1914

"HOME SWEET HOME." A DARTMOOR COTTAGE. 19428

110 *Left* Tavistock had been the seat of a mediaeval monastery and was one of the three *stannary* towns at which all the tin raised in Devon was checked and sold. In the second half of the nineteenth century the town flourished through its proximity to the Devon Great Consuls Mine, one of the richest copper mines in the world. The town centre bears the imprint of those years. Photograph: F. Frith & Co., 1893

112 *Right* In the 1850s, when the habit of leaving visiting cards at Cranmere Pool began, it was indeed a very remote place, approached with a guide from Chagford. The Mail Box, as it later became, was housed within the cairn, together with a visitors' book. Photograph: A. W. Searley

111 It was during the last decade of the nineteenth century that the first systematic study of Dartmoor's archaeological remains was made. Among those in the forefront of the campaign were Robert Burnard and his friend, the Reverend Sabine Baring-Gould, who is on the left of this group at Stall Moor Circle. Photograph: R. Burnard; April, 1894

113   *Top* Devon ponds do not often freeze hard enough to support the weight of skaters; still less frequently are skates readily available. This group was photographed at Peck Farm on the edge of Dartmoor. *c.* 1894

114   The use of the northern quarter of Dartmoor as an army training area has a long history. There has been an annual camp at Okehampton since 1875. In the photograph the Royal Horse Artillery pass through the centre of Okehampton, on a market day, before hauling their gun carriages up to the moor. 1894

THE NEW MACHINES

115   Valentine at the Exeter Control in the Aeroplane Race around Great Britain. "Imagine what people felt who saw the first steamboat, the first express train, the first motor car of modern make – and then the first aeroplanes" (*North Devon Journal*). Photograph: Chandler & Co., July, 1911

116 *Below* The *Queen* was the first locomotive to be used on the short Brixham Branch line. The engine had been bought from the contractors of the Portland breakwater. The enterprise was bought by the Great Western Railway in 1883. Photograph, 1868

117 *Above* The Torbay and Dartmouth Railway – ''A very serious accident occurred to the up train from Kingswear, fortunately without injuring any of the passengers, but resulting in the destruction of about 100' of line. The Gas Company were making a siding which had almost been finished. It is said that only half an hour's work was required to make it complete when the train came up'' (*Torquay Directory and South Devon Journal*). September, 1866

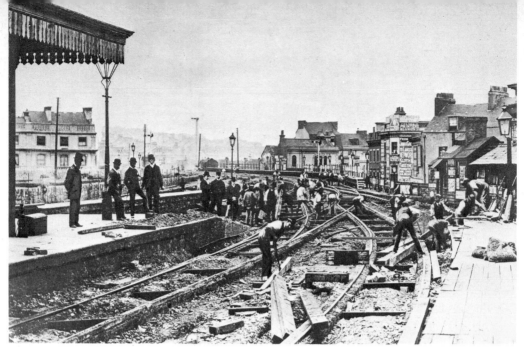

118 Conversion of gauge, Millbay Station, Plymouth. The South Devon Railway had reached Millbay in 1849; when the Great Western took over it decided to change the remaining broad and mixed gauge lines to narrow gauge throughout the region. It was a massive operation; 3,400 men were brought in to reinforce the local platelayers; sleeping accommodation was found in goods sheds and tents; they brought their own food. Here is the scene at Millbay as the lines were altered. May, 1892

119 Chelfham Viaduct, the largest engineering work of the narrow gauge, Barnstaple-Lynton railway; situated after an eight-and-a-half-mile climb from Barnstaple, the eight spans of the structure carried the track over the Stoke Rivers valley at a height of 72′. The construction of the railway worked out at twice the estimate and the company never raised enough capital to give it a good chance of success. Photograph: Major, Darker, and Loraine; 1897

120 The Meldon Viaduct which carried the railway around the western edge of Dartmoor; completed in 1874 the tallest of the cast-iron, latticed piers was 120′ high. Photograph: R. Burnard; September, 1890

121　The Bideford-Appledore railway. Terminal branches of railways have never been a financial success in north Devon. Opened in 1901, and a failure from the start, the track and rolling stock of this line were eventually put to good use behind the battle-front in France in 1917. Photograph: R. L. Knight, c. 1912

122　The untidy state of the track is evidence that this was the first train, carrying press reporters, on the Barnstaple-Lynton line. In the early days this observation car had no glass in its windows, the cords operated blinds. The engine is the Manning Wardle, *Taw*, built in Leeds. Photograph: Major, Darker, and Loraine; 1898

123　*Right* The opening of the Lynton-Lynmouth funicular. Originally intended to carry building materials from the harbour to the expanding village 500′ above. Sir George Newnes was one of the instigators of the project, as he was of the Barnstaple-Lynton railway; he stands on the platform of one of the cars. The funicular has no engine, only brakes; two cars, joined by an endless cable, are balanced by water ballast. Photograph: H. Montagu Cooper; May, 1898

124 The mountainous hills around Lynmouth were as much a challenge to the early motor cars as they were to horse-drawn vehicles. Dust, and the unstable road surfaces, were the main enemy of the car. *c.* 1912

125 A Wolseley, six horse-power, 1302cc, single-cylinder motor car, with wrap-round radiator, chain drive, three speeds and treadless tyres – photographed at Torquay when such machines were rarities. *c.* 1906

126 The Inauguration of the Exeter Electric Tramway system. The Mayor, E. C. Perry, at the controls of the first of a procession of decorated trams; a financial success, the trams contributed to the growth of suburban Exeter. Photograph: Heath & Bradnee; April, 1905

127 *Below* The first airman to arrive at Barnstaple arouses intense interest. ''Residents from the surrounding parishes flocked to the town and townsfolk turned out in their thousands. There was a roar of cheering as M. Salmet, a typical Frenchman with most affable manners, flew in over Codden at 1,000'''' (*North Devon Journal*). June, 1912

128 *Right* Installing the rails for Torquay's first tramways at the Strand. The Dolter system in which the current was passed through metal studs placed in the road between the running rails was used; it was not long before the following heading appeared in the *Torquay Directory* – ''Cab Horse Killed''; the unfortunate animal had been electrocuted by one of the studs. Photograph: *Torquay Times*, 1907

129 Chagford was one of the first centres used by visitors for the exploration of Dartmoor. The L.S.W.R., 12 m.p.h. motor bus evidently linked the village with exeter, but in 1908 the G.W.R. introduced a similar service to their closer railhead at Moretonhampstead. Photograph, *c.* 1905

VISITORS

130   At Two Bridges Hotel on Dartmoor; perhaps they had come on the day excursion which the G.W.R. had started in 1911. After leaving Paddington the first stop was Newton Abbot; after lunch at that town passengers left on a variety of tours one of which went to Two Bridges. The return train arrived at Paddington at 10.40 p.m. Note the first lady on the right carrying her compact, folding camera. 1912

131   Work in progress on two watercolours of the River Torridge and the ship repair yards at Appledore. All concerned were too interested in what they were doing to notice the approach of a somewhat shy man and, in any case, who would have known that the object, held under his arm, was a camera? Photograph: Paul Martin; 1894

132 Smile please! Little is known about these gentlewomen except that they were photographed at Torquay. Photograph: J. Stabb; *c.* 1905

133 *Left* Victoria Pavilion Ilfracombe; architect W. H. Gould. "An agreeable place in wet or inclement weather and in it are given daily concerts, the admission to which is free, built by the inhabitants to commemorate the Queen's Jubilee" (from a guide of the period). *c.* 1890

134 *Left below* Waiting at Clovelly harbour – the cameraman for subjects, the fishermen for herrings. The fish for which Clovelly had been famous early in the nineteenth century had greatly diminished in numbers by the time the village began to attract the attention of visitors in the 1860s – rather later than most places in north Devon. Photograph, 1913

135 *Below* Woolacombe hardly existed as a resort in 1880, but simple refreshments were available on the little Barricane beach where the shells, some of them brought across the Atlantic ocean by the Gulf Stream, were a source of interest. Visitors to Ilfracombe could buy a coloured version of this photograph in the early 1890s. Note the photographer reclining on the shingle. Photograph: Photochrom Co., *c.* 1890

136 *Below* Perhaps the dark haired woman and the seafaring man are the owners of the Ilfracombe guest house where the tables are laid for a dinner of wholesome, fresh food. *c.* 1890

137 *Right* Invalid carriages, drawn by donkeys or ponies, were available at Ilfracombe for transporting elderly visitors along the Torrs Walks and around the precipitous, cliff-hugging promenades. *c.* 1895

138 *Right below* The central lounge of the Valley of Rocks Hotel at Lynton; the cast-iron columns rose three floors and supported a beamed ceiling, infilled with coloured glass. In later days it reminded American guests of New Orleans. Photograph: F. Frith & Co., 1907

139 *Next page* Generations, of visitors and locals alike, have made use of the big flat rock on Wildersmouth beach; on the right the promenade wends its way round the silvery rocks of the Capstone. Photograph: Francis Bedford; *c.* 1880

140 Boys of the United Services College about to bathe from the pebble ridge at Westward Ho!
Rudyard Kipling, who had been at the school till 1882, was able to refer to his fellow pupils years later,
as "scattered throughout the five continents and the seven seas". Photograph: W. H. Puddicombe; *c.* 1895

NORTH DEVON

141 The ship-building and seafaring people of Appledore had the reputation of being a loyal, closely-knit community. The gentleman on the right side of Bude Street wears the uniform of the Devon Militia. Photograph: F. Frith & Co., 1906

142 *Below* Queen Anne's Walk, Barnstaple, situated on the quay before the construction of the Ilfracombe branch of the railway in 1873 cut it off from the river; till then this was the mercantile centre of the town. Under the canopy attached to the flagpole, a pair of scales were installed when required; the crates are of a type that was used for the transport of pottery. The figure on the left is thought to be the masonic tyler, the Lodge being situated behind the colonnade. *c.* 1860

143 *Right* Clovelly; only the clothes have changed, for which we have to thank the rigorous attitude of the owners, the Hamlyns. The donkey was widely used as a beast of burden in Devon at this date. Photograph: F. Frith & Co., 1890

144 Barnstaple, the *Tally Ho* about to leave for Lynton, a journey during which the coach had to be hauled over the 1,000′ contour; it was usual to harness two extra horses before the ascent of Loxhore Hill. Photograph: Major, Darker, and Loraine; *c.* 1895

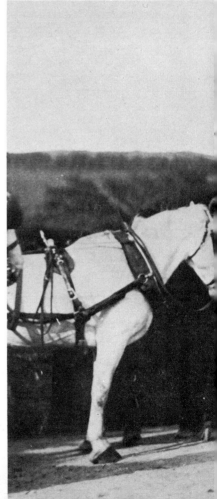

145 *Left* Great Torrington. The arcaded town hall had been built in 1861 and the Honourable Mark Rolle presented the gothic drinking fountain in 1870. Photograph: F. Frith & Co., 1894

146 Changing horse-power between Lynton and Ilfracombe. "All drivers engaged have many years experience", claimed the coach company. *c.* 1900

147 Ilfracombe; although for 20 years it had been possible to travel from Ilfracombe to Barnstaple by train, horse-drawn coaches continued to be used. The baths in the background date from Ilfracombe's first years as a resort in 1836. Photograph, 1896

148 Appledore; no quay existed here till 1844, when one was constructed at the end of the gardens, which, till then, extended to the water's edge. In these gardens the houses we see on the right of the photograph were then built. In Victorian times many Devon ports extended their quays

149 A Punch and Judy show at Wildersmouth Beach, Ilfracombe. A very similar photograph was made by Paul Martin. Photograph: J. Stabb, *c.* 1898

150   The *Mary* of Glasgow unloading Welsh coal on the old quay at Ilfracombe

151 Great Torrington; the church of St Michael, built in the style of the fifteenth century, was in fact constructed in 1651 to replace the one blown up, when it held 200 royalist prisoners, during the Civil War. Photograph: F. Frith & Co., 1890

152 St. Peter's Fair at Holsworthy probably attracted travelling people on account of the horse sale. It was customary for them to gather there and after the annual *Pretty Maid* ceremony couples were married at the church. This wedding group shows Sally Penfold and her groom, an Orchard; father-in-law Joe Orchard stands second from the left. *c.* 1910

153 *Below* Mr and Mrs A. W. Coles in Simmons Park, Okehampton (1907). Mr Coles later became mayor of Okehampton. The picture was taken, a few months after their marriage, by Mr Coles' sister, Miss R. Coles.

Lundy

154 The Manor Farm Hotel on Devon's tempestuous, off-shore island – Lundy. Throughout the period the island, whose population was considerably higher then than at present, maintained a certain independence of mainland affairs. Photograph: F. Frith & Co., 1896

155 The 14,000 ton Admiral class battleship *Montagu* went aground near the Shutter Rock, Lundy, at 2.00 a.m. in dense fog. She had been built at Devonport only three years before at a cost of £1,250,000; strenuous efforts were made to refloat her, but with her bottom pierced in several places, and both propellors snapped off, she became a total loss. May, 1906